A Character Building Book™

Learning About Courage from the Life of

Christopher Reeve

Jane Kelly Kosek

The Rosen Publishing Group's
PowerKids Press™
New York

For Christopher Reeve and all people who have the courage to fight for what they believe in
Special thanks to my superb editor Nancy Siegfried Ellwood

For information about paralysis and the Christopher Reeve Foundation please contact:
The Christopher Reeve Foundation, PO Box 277, FDR Station, New York, NY, 10150-0277, (888) 711-HOPE

Published in 1999 by The Rosen Publishing Group, Inc.
29 East 21st Street, New York, NY 10010

First Edition

Book Design: Erin McKenna

Photo Credits: pp. 4, 20 © Reuters/Fred Prouser/Archive Photos; p. 7 © Mark Solomon/Corbis-Bettmann; p. 8 © Steve Sands/AP Photo; p. 11 © M. Ferguson/The Gamma Liaison Network; p. 12 © Loren Fisher, Jersey Photographic Project/The Gamma Liaison Network; p. 15 © Marko Shark/Corbis-Bettmann; p. 16 © Einhorn/The Gamma Liaison Network; p. 19 © Markel/The Gamma Liaison Network.

Kosek, Jane Kelly.
    Learning about courage from the life of Christopher Reeve / by Jane Kelly Kosek.
        p.   cm. — (A character building book)
    Includes index.
    Summary: A brief biography of the actor famous for playing Superman, discussing his life before and after the accident that paralyzed him and focusing on the courage he has shown.
    ISBN 0-8239-5346-7
    1. Reeve, Christopher, 1952– —Juvenile literature. 2. Actors—United States—Biography—Juvenile literature. 3. Quadriplegics—United States—Biography—Juvenile literature. 4. Courage—Juvenile literature. [1. Reeve, Christopher, 1952– . 2. Actors and actresses. 3. Quadriplegics. 4. Physically handicapped. 5. Courage.] I. Title. II. Series.
PN2287.R292K67 1998
791.43'028'092—dc21
    [B]
                                                                                                            98-22106
                                                                                                            CIP
                                                                                                            AC

Contents

Forever a Superman

Superman is a superhero from comic books. Superman fights for truth and **justice** (JUS-tis). It takes a lot of **courage** (KUR-ij) for Superman to fight for what he believes in. Christopher Reeve knows this. Chris is an actor who played Superman in four movies. Like Superman, he has a lot of courage. After an injury in 1995 left him **paralyzed** (PA-ruh-lyzd), Chris found the courage to keep fighting for what he believes in and to help people lead better lives.

◀ *Chris knows that, even though he is paralyzed, people will always think of him as a Superman.*

5

A Love for Acting Is Born

Chris was born on September 25, 1952, in New York City. His parents **divorced** (dih-VORST) when he was only three years old. Chris took turns living with his mom and dad. When he was nine years old, he started acting. Chris found that acting helped him deal with his feelings about his family. Acting gave him courage. He also realized that acting was what he wanted to do most, and he was good at it. Chris dreamed of becoming a **professional** (proh-FEH-shuh-nul) actor.

Chris always liked being on the stage. ▶

Becoming a Serious Actor

While in high school, Chris acted in many plays. After high school, he continued to study acting at Cornell University. For his senior year of college, Chris wanted to study at The Juilliard School—one of the best **drama** (DRAH-muh) schools in the world. He knew that only two or three students would get into the advanced program at Juilliard. He was very nervous to **audition** (aw-DIH-shun), but he did a great job. He was accepted, along with a student who would become his close friend. That student was actor Robin Williams.

Chris and Robin have been friends since they met at Juilliard in 1973.

Playing Superman

After a year of hard work at Juilliard, Chris worked on a television show and acted in a play with the famous actress Katharine Hepburn. He was becoming well known. In 1977 he got the lead part in the movie *Superman*. When the movie opened, Chris became famous around the world. He used his fame to help people. Dressed as Superman, Chris would visit sick children in the hospital to cheer them up. He also helped needy children and fought for many **causes** (CAW-zez) with other artists.

Chris would go on to play Superman in three more Superman movies. ▶

Chris Gets Hurt

After the *Superman* movies, Chris was offered parts in many other movies. He always chose the most **challenging** (CHA-len-jing) ones. Chris loved sports as well as acting. He rode horses. He was a sailor and a pilot. He even flew alone across the Atlantic Ocean twice. Chris was always careful whenever he played sports. But in May 1995, he was thrown from his horse, Buck, during a riding event. Chris fell on his head and broke his neck. He couldn't breathe or move his body. Chris was scared.

◀ *Riding horses was always one of Chris's favorite things to do.*

The Operation

After Chris fell, people had to work quickly to help him breathe. Then they rushed him to the hospital. He needed an **operation** (ah-puh-RAY-shun) to **survive** (ser-VYV). Chris was afraid. No one had ever done an operation like the one he needed. And there was a chance that he might not live through it. But Chris found the courage to fight for his life. And he survived the operation.

Now Chris is in a wheelchair. He needs a special machine to help him breathe. ▶

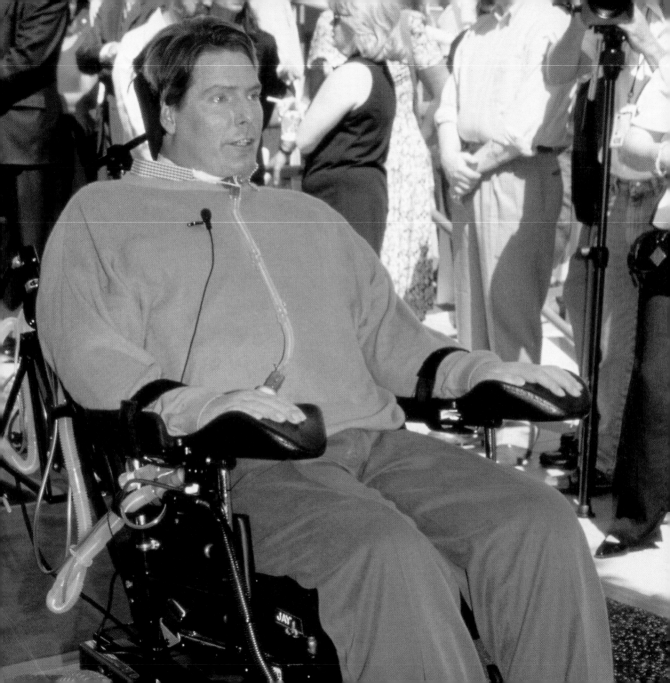

Rehabilitation

Even after the operation, Chris wasn't ready to go home. He had to enter a **rehabilitation** (REE-uh-bih-luh-TAY-shun) center. He chose a center that was close to his family so that he could spend time with them and have their support. The people at the center worked with Chris's body so that it would stay strong. They helped Chris breathe on his own for short periods of time. They also taught Chris how to work his new wheelchair.

◀ *Chris's wheelchair moves when he blows into a special tube.*

Having Courage Every Day

Every day Chris must deal with the fact that he can't move his body or breathe without help. He fights fear, anger, and sadness all the time. His family and friends help him have the courage to keep going. His wife, Dana, told him, "You're still you. And I love you." Those words reminded Chris that he is still the same person he always was. With love and support from his family and friends, he finds the courage and strength to get up and work hard every day.

Chris goes to events to speak about health care for people who are paralyzed. ▶

Doing What He Loves

Even though Chris is in a wheelchair, he is still able to do many things that he loves, including acting and directing. In 1996 Chris acted in a TV movie and **directed** (dih-REK-ted) a film called *In the Gloaming*. He loved directing. The film got wonderful **reviews** (rih-VYOOZ). It was even **nominated** (NAH-mih-nay-ted) for awards. That same year, Chris spoke in front of his fellow actors at the Academy Awards.

Chris received a star on the Hollywood Walk of Fame for all of his hard work in the theater, movies, and on television.

Finding a Cure

Chris's goal is to walk again. Scientists want Chris to reach that goal. They're trying to find a cure for paralysis. Chris has helped by giving speeches and forming the Christopher Reeve Foundation. This foundation raises money for **research** (REE-serch) and programs that help **disabled** (dis-AY-buld) people. He is also the chairperson of the American Paralysis Association and helped start the Reeve-Irvine Research Center. Chris is hoping that doctors will find a cure soon. But no matter what, Chris will stay strong and courageous.

Glossary

audition (aw-DIH-shun) To try out for something.

cause (CAWZ) Something that a person believes in and supports.

challenging (CHA-len-jing) Taking an effort to complete.

courage (KUR-ij) Strength that comes from inside a person to keep going.

direct (dih-REKT) To tell the actors what to do in a movie.

disabled (dis-AY-buld) Unable to do something.

divorced (dih-VORST) When a married couple is no longer married.

drama (DRAH-muh) Having to do with writing and acting in plays.

justice (JUS-tis) Fairness.

nominate (NAH-mih-nayt) To suggest that someone or something should be given an award.

operation (ah-puh-RAY-shun) A way to fix diseases and injuries.

paralyzed (PA-ruh-lyzd) Not being able to feel or move.

professional (proh-FEH-shuh-nul) An actor who gets paid to act.

rehabilitation (REE-uh-bih-luh-TAY-shun) Trying to make someone healthy again.

research (REE-serch) To study something very closely.

review (rih-VYOO) An opinion about a performance.

survive (ser-VYV) To keep living.

Index